The Legend of Dave the Villager 35

By Dave Villager

www.davethevillager.com
www.facebook.com/davevillager

Email me at: davevillagerauthor@gmail.com

BOOK THIRTY-FIVE:

Boggo's Wedding

THE STORY SO FAR…

Dave and his friends are reaching the end of their quest. The mysterious Bedrock City is only a few weeks walk away, and that's where they're hoping to find a portal to reach the End: the mysterious dimension that no one has been to for thousands of years.

After defeating Mad Mulligan and his forces, Dave hoped that his troubles were over, but then a nether portal appeared next to the house he and his friends were sleeping in. Fearing that the evil ruler of the Nether, the Empress, had returned, Dave prepared for the worst, but instead a lone piglin came out of the portal. A piglin who Dave knew very well.

It was Boggo.

Boggo invited Dave and the others to his wedding and asked Carl to be his best man. For a moment, it looked as if Dave and his friends were going to attend a fun event, without any bad guys attacking or weird things happening.

But then Boggo turned into a zombie.

Now Dave and his friends have to bring Boggo back to the Nether, to see if there's any way they can cure him…

CHAPTER ONE

The Groom

"Have you got him secure?" Dave asked.

"Yep," said Carl. "This little pig isn't going anywhere."

"ROKK!" snorted Boggo.

Carl was back in his golem suit and was holding Boggo under his arm. The piglin, who was now a zombie with moldy flesh and bits of bone showing, was struggling but wasn't strong enough to break free from Carl's grip.

"I must say, I do object to you calling Boggo a 'little pig,'" said Porkins. "That's a bit offensive, old chap."

"How about 'little piglin'?" Carl asked. "Is that less offensive?"

"Everyone, just be quiet a moment," said Dave. "Now come on — let's bring Boggo back to the Nether and see if there's any way to fix him."

"To be honest, I don't see much difference," said Spidroth. "He was a fool before he even became a zombie."

"I agree that Boggo isn't the sharpest tool in the chest, but we still have to help him if we can," said Dave. "Especially as he's supposed to be getting married."

"And Carl is going to be the best man," grinned Porkins. "You'd better hurry up and write a speech, old chap."

"I can help you write some jokes for the speech," said Alex. "People are always laughing at me, so I must be funny."

"Pah," said Carl.

"Come on," said Dave, walking towards the portal. "Let's go and see what we can do for Boggo."

"*BURR,*" said Boggo.

"Maybe Boggo's wife-to-be won't notice the difference," said Carl, looking down at the zombified piglin. "As Spidroth said, he's not that different than he was before. If anything, he sounds a bit more intelligent like this."

I can't believe there's another distraction to stop us from getting to the End, Dave thought to himself. He knew that they had to help Boggo, but he couldn't help feeling a bit disappointed. They were so close to an end portal now — only a few weeks away if Mad Mulligan could be believed. They were finally reaching the end of their quest, and Dave was eager to reach the End, and finish the mission he'd started all that time ago.

"Here we go," said Dave, taking out his diamond sword. Because they didn't know what kind of reception they would face in the Nether, he was wearing his netherite armor. Porkins was wearing a set of diamond armor, Carl had his golem suit, and Spidroth and Alex, as usual, weren't wearing any armor at all. Both of them were such good fighters that they rarely wore armor, as they could move much more freely without it. Dave agreed that sometimes armor could be a bit clunky, but he felt much safer with it on. Maybe once he became an expert with the Sight, he would feel safe enough not to wear any armor at all, but he preferred to have it on for now.

"Come on, hurry up," Carl said to Dave. "Let's get this over with."

Dave took a deep breath and walked through the Nether portal.

CHAPTER TWO

The Bride

Dave walked through the nether portal and emerged in a large room with purple nether brick walls. There were lots of strange screens and contraptions around the room, many of them making whirring sounds; it was obviously some kind of laboratory. Standing in front of the portal was a piglin in a wedding dress.

"Saggo?" said Spidroth, who had just walked through the portal after Dave.

"Hello Dave, hello Spidroth!" said Saggo happily. "Saggo pleased to see you!"

Then Carl stepped through the portal with Boggo under his arm, and Saggo's smile disappeared.

"Boggo!" she yelled, running over to him. Carl held up a netherite golem hand and held her back.

"You don't want to get too close to him," Carl said. "Not unless you want to get turned into a zombie as well."

Saggo began to sob.

"My poor Boggo!" she blubbed.

"Hi, I'm Alex; nice to meet you!" said Alex, oblivious that Saggo was crying.

"Don't worry, Saggo, we'll fix Boggo," said Dave.

"Gold apples and splash potions of weakness were unable to turn zombie pigmen back to normal, but perhaps they might work on zombie piglins?" Porkins suggested. "There are over a million years of evolution between pigmen and piglins, so our biology has to be quite different."

"I'm afraid that won't work," said a cheery female voice. At first, Dave couldn't see where the voice was coming from, and then he noticed a silver robot with glowing pink eyes. The robot was in the shape of a pigman — or rather, a pig woman.

"This is P1Go," said Saggo. "This is robot that helped me and Boggo get Empress's machine working."

"You were built by Chops?" Porkins asked the robot.

"Yes," said the silver robot. "Chops, or the Empress as she preferred to be known, built me as her own personal assistant. I was by her side for almost one million years before she left the Nether."

"Left the Nether?" said Carl, raising an eyebrow. "That's one way of putting it. She was blown to smithereens."

"If you say so, sir," said P1Go.

"So P1Go, are you saying that using a splash potion of weakness and a golden apple won't turn Boggo back to normal?" asked Dave.

"Yes," said the robot. "That treatment has proven to be ineffective in curing zombified piglins."

"Why did Boggo turn into a zombie anyway?" Carl asked.

"The Empress speculated that piglins who stayed in the Overworld too long would turn into zombies due to their bodies not being used to the colder environment," said the robot.

"Fool, we've seen other piglins go to the Overworld without turning into

9

zombies," said Spidroth. "The Empress sent an army of piglins to capture us when the Nether stopped fast-forwarding, and none of them turned into zombies."

"Yes, ma'am, but that was because the Empress administered them all with a special potion," said P1G0. "The potion allowed them to stay in the Overworld for several hours without a zombie transformation taking place."

"Wait," said Saggo, wiping the tears from her eyes, "you knew Boggo would turn into zombie, but you didn't tell us?!"

"You never asked, ma'am," said P1G0.

"Poor Boggo," sobbed Saggo. "He just wanted to come to Overworld to ask Carl to be his best man. Carl was Boggo's best friend. Best friend in all the world."

"Er... Yeah, of course," said Carl.

"P1G0, is there any way we can turn Boggo back?" Dave asked.

"Let me check my databanks," said the silver robot. For a few seconds, the lights in her pink eyes flickered, and then they turned back to normal again. "Yes, there is. Years ago, the Empress developed a special potion that could transform zombified piglins back into regular piglins. She abandoned the project as most zombified piglins were born as zombies, so even if you turned them into piglins, they rarely had the power of speech of cognitive thought. However, the potion was found to be 100% effective in all cases."

"Well, give us some of that potion then, rust for brains," said Carl.

"I'm afraid it is not that easy," said P1G0. "The laboratory where the Empress kept that potion is far away from here, in a location heavily affected by the zombie plague."

"What's the *zombie plague?*" Alex asked.

"Recently, zombified piglins have been causing trouble in the Nether on an unheard-of scale," said P1G0. "Normally, zombified piglins only get violent when they are attacked, but recently they have been attacking unprovoked. Some areas have become completely inhospitable to regular piglins. As of yet, I have yet to deduce the source of this plague."

"So zombified piglins are going crazy, and we're going to have to go to an area with loads of them," said Carl. "That's just great."

"That not great," said Saggo. "That very bad."

"I believe Carl was using a form of speech known as sarcasm, ma'am," said P1G0. "When he claimed that this situation was *great,* he actually meant the opposite. Isn't that right, Carl?"

"This robot better not be coming with us," said Carl. "Her shtick is going to get old real fast."

"Don't worry, Saggo," said Dave, putting a hand on the piglin's shoulder. "My friends and I are going to go to that other laboratory and fix Boggo. You'll still have your wedding, I promise."

"Saggo hopes so," sobbed the piglin. "Saggo already paid for catering."

CHAPTER THREE

The Venue

Before they left on their quest, Saggo wanted to check on the wedding preparations. Dave told her that she didn't need to come with them on the quest, but she insisted.

"Boggo is love of Saggo's life," she said defiantly. "Saggo must help save him."

Saggo didn't want to alarm any of the guests for fear that it would ruin the wedding, so they had to keep Boggo's condition secret.

The wedding was taking place outside in a warped forest biome, so Carl stayed with Boggo behind a large blue-green mushroom as the others joined Saggo to check on the ceremony.

The wedding was much larger than Dave expected, with crimson wood tables and chairs set out for the meal and rows of crimson wood seats for the wedding ceremony itself. Many piglins were busy decorating.

"Dave!" said a piglin, walking over to them. "Wroxo glad to see you!"

"Er, good to see you too, Wroxo," said Dave. The good thing about piglins was that they always said their own name out loud, so even if you didn't remember which one was which, you could soon work it out. Dave would have hated to admit it, but all the piglins looked pretty much the same to him

12

– even the women.

"Where is Boggo and Carl?" asked another piglin. "Groggo want to see Carl. Carl Groggo's good friend."

"Boggo and Carl are working on their speeches for the ceremony," said Porkins. "You chaps are really in for a treat — they are jolly good speeches."

"Groggo no like speeches," said Groggo. "Speeches boring. Groggo looking forward to wedding meal. Groggo likes eating."

"Wroxo likes eating too," said Wroxo. "But Wroxo likes dancing too. Wroxo hoping that pretty piglin girl will dance with him. Then maybe next wedding will be Wroxo's."

"No one will marry Wroxo," said Groggo. "Wroxo is not handsome like Groggo."

"Groggo no handsome!" said Wroxo. "Wroxo handsome. Dave, who is more handsome — Wroxo or Groggo?"

"Er, you're both equally handsome," said Dave. Technically he wasn't lying — he thought both piglins looked pretty much the same.

Saggo walked over to a piglin who was cooking something in a smoker.

"Saggo have to go get ready for a few hours," Saggo told the piglin. "But Saggo will be back in time for ceremony with Boggo."

"Zaffro will look after things until then," said the piglin at the smoker, who Dave realized was female.

"Thank you, Zaffro," said Saggo. "You are good friend."

The two piglins hugged, then Saggo walked back to join Dave and the others.

"Ceremony is soon," said Saggo. "We must hurry and fix Boggo."

"Fix Boggo?" said a voice. "What do you mean?"

Dave turned and saw another piglin behind them.

"Hello, Dave and Dave's friends," said the piglin. "Poffo glad to see you again."

Dave couldn't recall ever meeting Poffo before, but to be polite, he said: "Hello, Poffo. Great to see you."

"Is anyone else a bit confused?" Alex whispered. "All these piglins look really similar, and they all have similar names as well."

"And they're all similarly stupid," whispered Spidroth.

"Poffo ask again," said Poffo. "Why did Saggo say Saggo needs to fix Boggo? What is wrong with Boggo?"

Saggo sighed.

"Saggo tell Poffo secret, but Poffo must not tell anyone else. Agreed?"

Poffo nodded. Saggo told Poffo what had happened to Boggo and about their mission to go to the laboratory to get the potion.

"Poffo come too," said Poffo. "Poffo didn't help when Boggo tried to rebel against Empress. Poffo make big mistake then, and Poffo want to make up for it. Please let Poffo come?"

"Dave, can Poffo come?" Saggo asked.

"Er, yeah," said Dave. "The more, the merrier."

"Thank you, Dave," said Poffo. "Poffo will be brave. Brave like hoglin."

"Come on, that's enough messing about," said Spidroth. "If we're going to save your husband and get him back in time for the wedding, we need to get moving."

"Saggo agree," said Saggo.

"You might want to change out of that wedding dress, Saggo," said Alex. "It's not really an appropriate outfit for an adventure."

"Saggo keep wedding dress on," said Saggo. "It took Saggo long time to get on. Wedding dress complicated. Saggo no have time to take off and get changed."

"It must be so cool and romantic getting married," grinned Alex. "Is it cool and romantic, Saggo?"

"It was cool and romantic," said Saggo, "before Saggo's husband-to-be turned into zombie. Husband-to-be turning into zombie isn't very romantic."

"No," said Alex. "I suppose it's not."

CHAPTER FOUR

Death From Above

They rejoined Carl and Boggo and then made their way through the warped forest biome, with P1G0 leading the way. Even though she'd been built by the Empress, the silver pig woman robot seemed friendly enough.

In total, there were nine in their party: Dave, Carl, Spidroth, Porkins and Alex, the three piglins, Saggo, Poffo and Boggo (who was still a zombie and had to be held under Carl's arm) and P1G0. Dave would have preferred if he and his friends had gone alone, leaving the piglins behind, but Saggo and Poffo insisted on coming, and they had to bring Boggo as P1G0 wasn't sure if the potion had to be drank fresh or not.

"Have you been to this laboratory before?" Dave asked the silver robot.

"Oh yes," said P1G0. "As the Empress's assistant, I went with her to all her different bases and laboratories. She was always working on plans to get revenge on the Overworld."

"She sure was one crazy lady," said Carl.

"That crazy lady was a good person once," said Porkins, a sad look crossing his face. "But a lot of bad things happened to her, and the poor thing couldn't handle it."

"A lot of bad things have happened to me," said Carl, "and to you, and to all of us. But you don't see any of us turning into evil supervillains."

"I suppose not," said Porkins.

"Sometimes, there can be a fine line between what makes someone a good person or a bad person," said Spidroth. "Trust me, I know."

Dave thought about Robo-Steve and how he'd almost become a villain who'd wanted to rule the world. The Robo-Steve who Dave knew had been kind and gentle, but Future Dave, a version of Dave from an alternate timeline, had known a different Robo-Steve — a Robo-Steve who had caused countless death and suffering.

Suddenly they reached the end of the warped forest biome, and Dave was shaken from his thoughts. In front of them was a huge river of lava.

"How are we going to cross this?" Alex asked.

"We ride striders," said Saggo, pointing at some red creatures wading in the lava.

"Wow," said Alex, "those things are cool — they can walk in lava without burning up!"

Dave was surprised to hear that Alex had never seen a strider before, but he supposed that they hadn't been in existence very long. It had only been a few weeks, or maybe months (Dave had lost track of time) since the Nether had fast-forwarded, changing beyond all recognition. The old Nether had been a barren place full of endless netherrack and lava, but the new Nether contained different biomes and strange new creatures like these striders. Dave had ridden on the back of a strider before, but he wasn't looking forward to repeating the experience. Even though riding striders seemed safe enough, he still didn't like the idea of crossing lava on the back of some strange creature.

Saggo reached into her white dress and pulled out a handful of fishing rods.

"Saggo sneak these away from wedding," the piglin said proudly. "Warped fungus on stick was for wedding guests to cross lava river to see fireworks, but fixing Boggo more important."

She handed them each a fishing rod. Dave saw that each rod had a blue-green mushroom with orange spots on the end of it — warped fungus.

"Cool," said Alex, looking at her rod. "Do those strider things like these mushrooms then?"

"Striders love warped fungus," said Saggo. She walked to the edge of the lava river and dangled her rod towards the striders, shaking the warped fungus on the end of it. "Dinnertime striders! Come get dinner from Saggo!"

The striders quickly spotted the warped fungus and walked over towards Saggo. Dave had seen striders before, but he still couldn't get used to them — they were such unique creatures, unlike anything else in the Nether or the Overworld. Bright red, their bodies were large squares with far apart eyes, drooping mouths and wisps of thin, string-like hair on their temples. They had no arms, just two long red legs. The bottom of their legs were grey and crusty, which Dave supposed came from a lifetime of walking in lava.

Saggo walked backward, forcing the striders to come on land to get the fungus. The striders hesitated a moment, then walked out of the lava. Immediately their skin turned purple, and they began to shiver.

"Striders don't like being out of lava," Poffo said. "Striders get cold."

How the striders could ever be cold in the Nether, where it was always warm, Dave had no idea. He supposed that if they normally lived in lava, they were used to quite high heats.

Saggo put her warped fungus on a stick away before the striders could get it, then she pulled some saddles out from somewhere in her dress and placed them on the striders. Once all the striders had saddles, she turned towards Dave and the rest of the group.

"You can ride striders now," she told them. "Get on saddles and use warped fungus to guide them."

"Oh, I get it," said Alex. "It's like using a carrot on a stick to guide a pig."

"Saggo no know what is carrot on stick," said Saggo. "Saggo no know what is pig."

Even though Alex had never ridden a strider before, she easily clambered onto hers, and within seconds was guiding it around using the warped fungus on the end of the fishing rod.

"This is fun!" she said happily, then she walked her strider straight into lava, without a care in the world.

"Er, how am I going to ride a strider?" Carl asked. "The last time I rode one of those things, I didn't have my golem suit — thanks to Boggo."

"Just get on strider and ride," said Saggo.

"My golem suit might be a bit heavy for it," said Carl. "It is too heavy for horses."

"Saggo no know what is horse, but strider is strong," said Saggo. "Strider can carry Carl."

"If you say so," said Carl reluctantly. "But don't blame me if I squish this strider flat."

Carl still had Boggo under his arm, but his golem suit was so tall that he easily climbed onto the strider's saddle without needing to pull himself up. For a moment, the strider wobbled, but then it seemed perfectly fine. As Saggo had said, it was able to take Carl's weight, and Carl was sitting on it with no problem.

"Saggo told Carl," grinned Saggo. "Strider strong."

"So, this is what riding feels like," said Carl, with a grin. "It's kind of cool."

Keeping Boggo under one arm, Carl held the warped fungus on a stick in the other hand, dangling it in front of his strider. The strider walked forward, walking into the lava.

"Carl be careful not to drop Boggo in lava," said Saggo, giving Carl a concerned look.

"I make no promises," said Carl.

"BURR," said Boggo.

Everyone else had led their striders into the lava now, so Dave did the same, dangling the warped fungus out in front of it using his fishing rod.

"CRRURP," said the strider, then it walked forward. As the strider began walking across the lava, Dave could feel the heat all around him.

Just one slip-up, and I'll be dead, Dave thought, looking down at the lava all around him. He knew he was secure on the saddle, but it didn't stop him from feeling scared. He didn't think he'd ever get used to riding across lava, no matter how many times he did it.

"Come on," said Saggo. "Follow Saggo."

Saggo began leading her strider across the lava lake, and the others follow behind her. As they got closer to the opposite shore, Dave saw that it was a basalt delta biome — a bleak gray biome made from hills of basalt and blackstone. Of all the new Nether biomes, it was certainly the least welcoming.

"Isn't there a more scenic route we can take?" Carl asked. "Those basalt biomes aren't very inviting."

"There are altenate routes, sir, but they will take much longer," said P1Go.

"So how come you're good now anyway?" Carl asked the robot. "Or is this one big evil plan to lead us into a trap?"

"I am neither good nor bad," said P1Go. "I am programmed to obey orders and offer assistance. My primary function is to serve the Empress above all others, but because she's gone now, I can serve anyone who asks me for assistance."

"Dear boy, when you say 'gone,' you do mean 'dead,' don't you?" Porkins asked. "The Empress is dead, isn't she?"

"I do not believe so," said P1Go. "The last time I saw her, she was starting to build a new golem army amongst the ruins of her castle, then she disappeared. My scanners have been unable to detect here, so I suspect she has left the Nether."

Dave didn't like that news one bit. He and the others had believed the Empress had died when Steve had destroyed her castle, but it looked like she'd survived. Whatever she was up to, he was sure that it was nothing good.

Finally, they reached the shore of the basalt delta biome. They walked their striders up onto the land and climbed off the saddles. The striders were all purple and shivering. Saggo reached into her pockets and pulled out some warped fungus, throwing them to the striders, who caught the mushrooms in their mouths.

"You go now, striders," she said. "Saggo grateful for striders' help."

The striders all walked off back into the lava, where their skin immediately became red again and they stop shivering.

"Riding those things was fun," said Alex. "They're like lava horses."

"What is horse thing everyone keeps talking about?" said Saggo, looking very confused.

"Come on," said Dave. "We should get a move on."

Saggo walked over to Boggo, who was still zombified and held underneath Carl's golem arm.

"Don't worry, Boggo," Saggo said softly. "We fix you soon."

"RURRK," said Boggo.

They began their journey across the basalt delta. Unlike the warped forest biome, where they could walk casually through it, the hills of the delta were so steep that they had to climb most of the way, squeezing between gaps and clambering up and down jagged peaks. Before long, Dave's arms and legs were aching from the strain. It didn't help that the air was thick with fog and ash, making it difficult to breathe. They had to go slowly, as there were constant drops and chasms, many of them with lava down below. There were lava waterfalls as well, the orange liquid pouring from the gray ceiling of the biome, high above them.

They were clambering across a particularly steep hill when Alex held up a hand, indicating that they should all be quiet.

"Can you hear that?" she whispered.

Dave could hear it too now, a thudding sound coming from somewhere above them. He looked up, and for a moment, he couldn't see anything, just jagged peaks of basalt and blackstone above them, but then a huge square creature bounded into view on a cliff above them.

"Magma cubes!" Poffo shouted, the panic rising in his voice.

The magma cube was a dark red color — so dark that it was almost black. Like a slime, its body was a perfect cube, with no arms and legs, just two glowing orange eyes.

The cube jumped and fell through the air towards them.

That thing is huge! Dave had time to think.

"Everyone scatter!" Spidroth screamed.

They all got out the way as best they could, which was difficult as they were on a jagged peak of rock without many places to go. Dave clambered down the rock face just in time as the magma cube landed above them. It was so heavy that the peak shook, and Dave almost lost his grip. He looked down and saw that there was a stream of lava far below him that he hadn't seen before. If he fell, he would be doomed.

The magma cube jumped again and fell straight towards Dave. This time there was nowhere for him to go – he was on a narrow crop of rock with nowhere to move to.

"Dave, grab my hand!"

Dave turned. It was Carl – the creeper was standing on a nearby ledge, holding out one of his golem arms for Dave. He was still a couple of blocks away, so Dave was going to have to jump. He took a deep breath, then leaped through the air, just as the magma cube smashed onto the ledge behind him. Dave grabbed hold of Carl's golem arm, clinging on for dear life. He looked behind and saw that the magma cube was too big for the ledge, and it toppled off, falling down into the lava below.

Carl lifted Dave and dropped him safely on the ledge next to him.

"Thanks, buddy," Dave said, wiping the sweat from his forehead.

"Don't thank me yet," said Carl, looking up. "Our troubles aren't over!"

Dave looked up and saw that Carl was right — more magma cubes were leaping off ledges above them, raining down from the sky.

"Everyone, keep moving!" Dave shouted. "We need to find shelter! We need to get out of here!

As the magma cubes fell down all around them, Dave and the others all made their way forward as fast as they could, clambering around jagged rocks while avoiding getting squished. Every time a magma cube landed, the ground shook, so they had to be careful not to lose their grip.

Dave was just about to jump from one steep spiral of rock to another when a magma cube fell through the air just in front of him. He breathed a deep sigh of relief – if he'd jumped any sooner, the cube would have landed on him in mid air and the two of them would have fallen into the lava pool below.

"Poffo no like adventures anymore!" whined Poffo, clinging on to the side of a jagged basalt pillar. "Poffo scared!"

Dave joined him on the pillar and put a hand on the piglin's shoulder.

"It's okay to be scared, Poffo," he said. "But we need to keep going if we're going to avoid getting squished."

To illustrate his point, a magma cube slammed into a pillar just above them. It turned to face them, then jumped again, falling right towards them.

"Jump!" Dave shouted.

Poffo jumped to the next pillar, and Dave jumped after him, both of them escaping just in time to avoid getting squished by the magma cube.

"There's a cave!" Alex shouted from somewhere ahead. Dave looked over and saw that she was far ahead of all of them. With her ninja skills, she'd been able to jump from pillar to pillar with ease. Behind Alex, Dave saw the entrance to a cave cut into the side of a huge gray mountain.

Up ahead, Poffo and Saggo were jumping from basalt spire to basalt spire, heading towards the cave, when suddenly, Saggo slipped. She fell and just managed to hold onto a ledge by the tips of her trotters. Far below her, a pool of lava surrounded the foot of the spire. If she fell, she would get fried.

"Help!" Saggo screamed. "Saggo no want to die!"

Spidroth, Alex and P1Go were ahead, and Carl and Dave were behind, and they all began rushing forward to help Saggo. But before they got there, Poffo reached down a trotter.

"Poffo save Saggo!" said Poffo. "Grab Poffo's trotter!"

Saggo reached down and grabbed Poffo, who then pulled her up. The two of them sat on the ledge, breathing heavily.

"Poffo save Saggo," said Saggo. "Poffo is hero."

Poffo blushed.

"Poffo just saving friend," said Poffo.

"Hurry up, fools," said Spidroth. "Get to the cave!"

They all rushed forward, jumping from spire to spire until all of them were safely in the cave. Dave looked out and saw that more magma cubes were raining from the sky, slamming into the pillars or landing straight in lava.

"I hate this biome," said Carl.

"How's Boggo doing?" Dave asked.

Carl looked down at the zombified piglin under his arm. Boggo still looked as gormless and zombified as before. Although Dave had to admit he was the smartest dressed zombie he'd ever seen — there weren't many zombies who wore wedding suits.

"I think he's fine," said Carl, "although he's starting to smell a bit. It must be all the moldy flesh."

"Poor Boggo," said Saggo, walking over to her husband-to-be. "Saggo will save you, my love. Saggo promise."

"Come on, you guys," said Alex, who had gone slightly ahead in the cave. "I think the basalt biome comes to an end here. I can see some kind of weird red forest up ahead."

"A crimson forest biome," said P1G0. "In general, those are far safer than basalt delta biomes."

"Well, as long as there aren't any giant cubes raining from the sky, that's good with me," said Carl. "Now, let's hurry this up — Boggo is really starting to stink."

CHAPTER FIVE

Zombified Piglins

After the chaotic spires, cliffs and lava pools of the basalt dealta biome, the crimson forest biome seemed like a haven. Giant crimson mushrooms grew all around them, many of them with strange lamp-like glowing blocks inside them that P1G0 said were called shroomlights. Red vines hung down from the giant mushrooms, and smaller mushrooms littered the ground. The ground itself was made from a squishy red material a bit like grass, called nylium.

Dave was starting to think that this biome would be a pleasant place to live, but then he caught sight of some hoglins in the distance — huge, pig-like creatures with fierce tusks. Dave had fought hoglins before and did not care to repeat the experience, so they kept as far away from the huge beasts as possible.

After walking for a while, they began to feel hungry. It was hard to know how much time had passed in the Nether since there were no days or nights, so Dave had no idea if it was actually lunchtime, but from the growling of his stomach, he guessed that it must be near. So they all picked some mushrooms, then Porkins and P1G0 cooked them in smokers. Dave was a little worried that the smell of cooking mushrooms might attract hoglins, but thankfully none of the huge beasts approached them. The group all sat down, eating their mushrooms and chatting.

Carl tried to feed Boggo some mushrooms, but the zombified piglin just spat them back out.

"HAHOO!" grunted Boggo.

"Zombified piglins do not need to eat," said P1Go. "At least regular zombified piglins don't."

"What do you mean, 'regular'?" asked Dave.

"Most zombified piglins aren't former piglins like Boggo," explained P1Go. "Most of them were born that way. For generations, zombified piglins have bred in the Nether, so most of the zombified piglins you see here have parents who are zombies as well. A regular piglin rarely gets bitten by a zombified piglin, as zombified piglins normally only attack when provoked."

"I'm not sure about that, old chap," said Porkins. "Every time I've bumped into zombified piglins, those blighters have always been jolly aggressive. They wiped out an army of illagers, and they tried to attack Carl, Alex and I as well."

"Yes, recently zombified piglins have been unusually aggressive in the Nether," said P1Go. "As I said before, I am currently unaware of what the reason for this is. But we should try to avoid zombified piglins if possible. They are fairly weak but usually congregate in vast numbers."

"We should avoid crazy zombie piglins," said Carl, "got it."

"Why did Boggo transform into a zombie?" Alex asked. "He wasn't bitten."

"As mentoned before, the Empress correctly theorized that piglins who went to the Overworld would transform into zombies," said P1Go. "That is why when she sent her piglin soldiers to capture your group, Steve and Herobrine, she gave the piglins a special potion to stop them from transforming. She also theorized that a hoglin that went to the overworld would become zombified as well."

"A zombie hoglin," said Carl. "I don't like the sound of that."

"The Empress called this theoretical creature a 'zoglin,'" said P1G0.

"That is a pretty cool name," said Carl. "I know the Empress was crazy and evil, but it sounds like she was good at naming stuff."

After they'd eaten, they started walking through the crimson forest again. Dave decided to make the most of his time in the forest by collecting some of the unique blocks and items. He used his diamond axe to chop some blocks of crimson wood from the stems of the huge mushrooms (P1G0 informed him that the proper name for the blocks was 'crimson stems' rather than 'crimson wood'). He also picked some of the red mushrooms with orange spots that littered the ground. P1G0 informed him that these crimson fungus were useful for breeding hoglins (although why anyone would want to breed hoglins, Dave had no idea) but that warped fungus, the cyan mushrooms with orange spots found in warped forest biomes, could be placed in plant pots to keep hoglins away, as the huge beasts had a strange aversion to them. Whenever a group of hoglins began to walk too close towards them, P1G0 would place some warped fungus down on the ground to keep them away.

Stiff, stringy plants called crimson roots grew on the ground as well, so Dave put some of them in his bag, even though P1G0 told him they didn't have many practical uses. He collected some of the crimson vines that hung down from the mushrooms as well. P1G0 was more positive about these, saying that they grew down from blocks if placed correctly and could be used as makeshift ladders.

Dave's favorite block in the crimson forest were the shroomlights. They were squishy orange cubes that grew on the underside of the giant mushroom cups, and they emitted light without being attached to a redstone circuit. Dave was sure they'd come in useful, so he tried to collect as many as possible.

The walk through the forest was so pleasant that Dave almost forgot that they were on a quest to save Boggo, and it was only the occasional *"BURR"* from Boggo that reminded him.

I could actually imagine living here, Dave thought to himself. *I could have a nice house made from crimson stem, with plant pots with warped fungus all around the house, to keep away the hoglins. If I had a nether portal next to my house, I could go back and visit the Overworld whenever I liked.*

It was just as Dave was in the middle of these pleasant daydreams that he heard a not so pleasant sound coming from his left. He turned and saw that something was going on in the distance.

"What's going on over there?" Spidroth asked, peering in the same direction. Some sort of creatures were moving towards them, but there were so many giant mushrooms and vines in the way that it was hard to see what they were.

Carl squinted. The creeper had the best eyesight out of any of them.

"Oh no," said Carl, his black eyes going wide. "Zombie piglins!"

"Their official name is zombified piglins," said P1Go.

"I couldn't care less what you call them," said Carl, "hundreds of them are coming this way!"

"Poffo run!" shouted Poffo before running off between the giant mushrooms.

"I think that fool has the right idea," said Spidroth. "Everyone run!"

They all began dashing through the forest, weaving their way past the giant mushrooms and around roots and vines. As they ran, Dave turned and saw that the zombified piglins were gaining on them. He'd never seen zombies moving that fast.

"Do zombified piglins always move that quickly?" Dave asked P1G0.

"No," said the robot. "Ever since they've become more aggressive, they seem to have become faster as well. It really is perplexing."

"Well, if they catch us, it's going to be perplexing how dead we are," said Carl.

"I do not believe that is a proper use of the word perplexing," said P1G0.

Carl rolled his eyes and kept on running.

Finally, they ran out of the crimson forest and found themselves on the shore of a huge lava river. On the other side of the river was a colossal black castle. It looked like it had been abandoned for some time, with parts of its towers broken in places. There was a narrow black bridge leading across the river to the castle.

"That's a bastion remnant," said P1G0. "One of the castles that used to be controlled by the Empress during the time of the Bastion Empire. They were abandoned long ago."

"Will it be safe in there?" Dave asked.

"I do not know," admitted the robot.

"Well, it will be safer than here," said Carl, turning around and looking at the zombified piglins rushing through the crimson forest towards them.

Dave had to agree. If they didn't escape now, zombified piglins were going to get them. He didn't like the look of the bastion remnant one bit, but there didn't seem to be any other choice.

"Come on, we'll cross the bridge and destroy it behind us!" Dave shouted.

They all ran towards the bridge. The bridge was long but only four blocks wide, with walls on either side to stop anyone from falling off into the lava. Dave and the others all ran across the bridge, crossing the lava river. When they reached halfway, Dave turned and pulled out some blocks of TNT. He placed the TNT across the bridge as quickly as he could.

"Everyone stand back!" Dave shouted. He pulled out some flint and steel and lit one of the TNT blocks. It flashed white. Dave ran away from the TNT as fast as he could, then heard it explode behind him.

KADOOOOOOM!!!!!!!

The explosion was so large that Dave was sent flying forward and landed on his front. He pushed himself to his feet and turned around. The bridge had broken, and the zombified piglins were on the other side, snorting angrily that they couldn't get across.

"See you later, losers!" Alex shouted at the zombified piglins.

"We will have to see them later," said P1Go. "We're going to have to come back this way when we return to the wedding."

"Oh," said Alex. "Er, sorry about calling you losers, guys. No hard feelings."

"Come on," said Dave, looking up at the huge black castle. "Let's make our way through this place as fast as we can. I don't like the look of it one bit."

"Saggo scared," said the piglin, looking up at the black castle. "When Empress alive, piglins used to go into bastion remnants and not come out. Bastion remnants scary places."

"I'm sure it will be fine," said Dave. "The Empress is gone now, remember?"

"Saggo suppose so," said Saggo, although she sounded very unsure. Dave was very unsure himself, but he tried to put on a brave face.

"Weapons at the ready," said Dave. "Let's make sure we're ready for whatever we find in here."

"I think that's a jolly good idea, old chap," said Porkins, looking up at the castle. "A jolly good idea indeed."

CHAPTER SIX

The Bastion Remnant

As they walked through the entrance to the colossal black castle, a chill went down Dave's spine. The bastion remnant was like something out of a horror movie, with black walls and lanterns hanging down from the ceiling with chains. The walls were made from black bricks, some of them cracked in places. They were in a large hallway, but there were gaps in the walls, the ceiling and the floor where they could see through to other rooms. Porkins almost fell into a hole in the floor, but thankfully P1G0 grabbed his arm just in time.

"Good gosh," said Porkins, looking down at the hole. "You save my bacon there, dear chap."

Dave walked carefully over and looked down into the hole. Below was a pool of lava. If P1G0 hadn't stopped Porkins, the pigmen would have fallen straight into it.

"Watch your footing, everyone," said Dave.

The layout of the bastion remnant was very confusing, with passages and stairways going off in lots of different directions. It was made all the more confusing by all the gaps in the walls, so it was hard to know where one hallway or staircase ended and another began.

"Wait," said Carl, who was walking slightly ahead of them, "is that gold?"

Dave walked over to him. Carl was looking at one of the black blocks in the wall that had thin lines of shiny yellow material running through it.

"Gold!" said Poffo excitedly. He pulled out a golden pickaxe and immediately began hacking at the block. Once he'd destroyed it, some gold nuggets fell to the ground. Poffo quickly picked them up and stuff them into his pockets.

"Was that some kind of gold ore?" Dave asked.

"Yes," said P1Go. "Those blocks are known as *gilded blackstone*. They sometimes appear in the walls of bastion remnants and are a good place to mine gold from."

Dave looked around and saw that there were other black blocks with veins of gold running through them. Poffo was running around, minding as much gold as he could. Dave had seen before that piglins liked gold, but it was as if Poffo was caught in some sort of frenzy – he was obsessed with getting every little bit of gold that he could. Dave turned around and saw that Saggo was looking at the gold with envious eyes. It was clear that she wanted to mine it too, but she managed to hold herself back.

"That's enough of that," said Spidroth, grabbing Poffo's pickaxe arm. "We are on a mission to save your friend, don't forget."

"Oh yeah," said Poffo, looking around at Boggo, who was still zombified and underneath Carl's arm. "Poffo forgot."

It was like Poffo had come out of a trance. He looked sleepy and was rubbing his head.

Piglins seem to be almost addicted to gold, Dave thought himself.

They walked on, weaving their way through narrow hallways, doing their best not to fall through gaps in the floor into pools of lava. Poffo finally seemed to be over his thirst for gold, but then they came across something that made the piglin's eyes go wide: a solid gold block right in the middle of one of the walls. Poffo dashed over and ran his trotters along the smooth gold surface. There were a couple of other gold blocks in the walls nearby as well, Dave saw.

"A solid gold block!" Poffo said, tears in his eyes. "Poffo always dream of having solid gold house!"

"Well, keep dreaming, pig face," said Carl, giving Poffo a light whack on the back of the head. Poffo immediately shook himself out of his trance, but he still couldn't keep his beady white eyes off the gold block.

They came around another corner, and this time there was a small wooden chest against one of the walls. Dave opened the chest and saw that it was full of a variety of different items and blocks. There were blocks of blackstone, a few tools made from both diamond and iron, some chains, some porkchops and a set of golden armor. Dave pocketed most of the items, but he gave the golden armor to Poffo.

"Thank you, thank you, thank you," said Poffo, quickly putting the armor on.

"Fool," said Spidroth. "Do you know how easily gold armor breaks?"

"Poffo no care," said Poffo. "Poffo look cool."

There was a spare golden helmet, so Dave gave it to Saggo. She looked very odd, wearing a full white wedding dress and a golden helmet on her head.

"Does Saggo look pretty?" she asked Dave.

"Er, yes, very pretty," said Dave. He noticed Spidroth giving him a suspicious look, so he quickly said: "let's keep moving, shall we?"

They walked down a short staircase and found themselves in a large open area, with several hoglins roaming about. There was a patch of brown soul sand on the ground with red nether wart growing out of it, and some of the hoglins were grazing on the nether wart. Like the rest of the castle, this area was ruined and decayed, with walls missing and gaps in the ceiling and floor. Looking around the room, Dave guessed it had once been a stable of some kind, with pens for the hoglins. The pens were all broken now, and the hoglins were roaming about wherever they pleased. Dave and the others kept as far away from the hoglins as they could, walking around the edge of the room and trying their best not to attract attention. A couple of the hoglins looked at them, but thankfully they didn't attack.

After walking through a few more broken hallways, they reached the biggest room they'd seen so far. It was a tall room, many stories high. Far below them, the floor of the room was covered in lava, with a few blackstone blocks placed in the lava in a grid pattern. Dave and the others were on one of the upper floors of the huge room. On the other side of the room, Dave spotted the first living creatures he'd seen since they'd entered the bastion remnant — some piglins wearing black rags. Each of them had a huge gold belt buckle and a strange gold gauntlet strapped to one of their arms. There were about five of them, and they were holding golden axes. They seem to be patrolling, walking back and forth around the room.

"Piglin brutes," whispered Saggo darkly. "Those are bad piglins."

"What's a piglin brute?" Alex asked.

"Piglin brutes were the Empress's top commandos," said P1Go. "They were highly trained warriors and very dangerous. The Empress trained them to obey her every command, and since her disappearance, most of them have stayed loyal, guarding her bases and castles for when she returns."

"Oh, come on," said Carl. "How dangerous can a few piglins be?"

"Do not underestimate them, sir," said P1Go.

"Piglin brutes very tough," whispered Poffo. "If they catch us, we in big trouble."

"More like 'pig trouble,'" said Carl, grinning.

Everyone looked around at him.

"What?" said Carl. "It was a funny joke. You lot just don't appreciate good humor."

The piglin brutes had gathered on a walkway on the right to have a chat, Dave saw. The path along the left side of the room was completely unguarded.

"Now's our chance," Dave whispered. "Come on."

Dave led the way, walking quickly and quietly along the walkway. He tried not to look down at the lava pool a few stories below them.

Who would build a massive room with a pool of lava at the bottom? Dave wondered. He couldn't see what practical use a room like this had, but everything in the bastion remnant was so decayed and ruined that maybe the room had made sense at some point.

Up ahead of them was a doorway. If they could reach the doorway before the piglin brutes saw them, they could leave the massive room safely. Dave glanced to his left and saw that the piglin brutes still hadn't noticed them.

Dave stood by the doorway, ushering the others through. Spidroth and Alex went through first, followed by Porkins, Saggo and Poffo, then P1G0 the robot, and finally Carl, with Boggo still under his arm. Carl ducked his head down and was just about to go through the doorway when Boggo let out a groan.

"HORR!"

Immediately, Dave heard angry snorts behind him. He turned and saw the piglin brutes on the other side of the room had finally noticed them. They had their golden axes in their hands and were rushing around the edge of the room towards them.

They may be tough, but there's only five of them, Dave thought, taking out his diamond sword. *We'll easily defeat them.*

Then he heard snorting behind him. He turned around and saw more piglin brutes rushing towards him from the other side of the room as well. Down on the other floors of the huge room, he could see piglin brutes running up staircases, all of them heading in the direction of him and Carl.

"It looks like we're going to be running for our lives again," said Carl. "Just like old times."

"It looks that way," agreed Dave. "RUN!!!"

CHAPTER SEVEN

Battle with the Brutes

Dave and Carl ran through the doorway, where the others were waiting for them in a ruined hallway.

"What's going on?" Alex asked. "What's all that snorting?"

"The piglin brutes are coming for us," said Dave. "And there are a lot of them."

Alex took out her two diamond swords, Spidroth took out her red sword, and Porkins notched an arrow on his bow.

"I've never been to a wedding before," said Carl, flexing his golem arms, "but I can confidently say that this is the worst wedding of all time."

"Carl, don't be rude about Saggo's wedding," said Saggo crossly.

"Come on," said Dave. "We need to get out of here."

Dave began running down the hallway, but then he heard snorts coming from up ahead of them. It seemed that the piglins were closing in on them on all sides.

"It looks like we don't have any choice but to fight," said Dave, gripping his diamond sword tightly. He wished he still had his old netherite blade, but that had been destroyed in the lava when Spidroth defeated Mad Mulligan.

Dave didn't have much faith that either Saggo or Poffo would be much use in the battle, but then he remembered P1Go.

"Can you fight?" he asked the robot.

"I do have self-defense protocols," said P1Go. "If I am attacked, I'm programmed to defend myself."

"Well, you're about to be attacked," said Carl. "So get defending."

A hatch slid open in the middle of the silver robot's chest, then P1Go reached inside and pulled out a netherite sword.

"Defense mode initiated," she said, holding the sword out in front of her. Her eyes began to glow red.

The horde of piglin brutes, all wearing black rags and holding golden axes, ran through the doorway, out of the large room that Dave and the others had just left. Simultaneously, a horde of piglin brutes ran towards them from the other end of the hallway.

To Dave's surprise, Poffo had taken out a netherite sword and was standing next to him, ready to fight the brutes.

"You know how to use a sword, Poffo?" Dave asked.

"Poffo was in Empress's army," said Poffo. "Poffo may not be as well trained as a piglin brutes, but Poffo can still fight."

Dave was even more surprised to see Saggo holding a crossbow. She looked quite the sight, in her white wedding dress and gold helmet.

"Saggo will defend her true love Boggo," said Saggo defiantly.

"Are you going to be all right fighting with Boggo under your arm?" Dave asked Carl.

I'll be fine," said Carl. "I only need one arm to beat up these bozos."

"*BURR,*" said Boggo.

"We need to defend from both directions," Dave told them all. "Carl, P1Go and Poffo, you stay on this side with me, and Spidroth, Alex, Porkins and Saggo, you four stay on the other side."

"Got it, old chap," said Porkins. "Let's give these blaggards a darn good thrashing. Pip pip, tally-ho, chocks away!"

"Porkins say funny words," said Saggo. "Does Porkins's brain work properly?"

"Here they come!" said Dave.

"Yes, I can see that," said Carl, rolling his eyes. "I am standing right next to you."

The piglin brutes rushed into them from either side, and the battle began. Immediately the brutes began hacking away at Dave with their golden axes, much more viciously than Dave would have expected. He raised his diamond sword to block the blows but was unable to block all of them. Thankfully, his netherite armor was able to block the blows as well, but the brutes were hitting him so fast that he wasn't sure how much more his armor would be able to take before it broke.

Next to him, Carl was swinging his right arm at the brutes, sending them flying, while continuing to hold Boggo under his left arm. However, after a few of them had been sent flying, the piglin brutes wisened up to Carl's attack strategy and began ducking out of the way of his arm swings, then rushing over and swinging their golden axes into the golem suit. Carl kicked and punched them away as best he could, but more of them kept coming.

Poffo was fighting surprisingly well, swinging his netherite sword to block the blows from the golden axes. However, a few of the brutes managed to hit him on his golden chest plate, and it broke, leaving his middle exposed.

"Poffo, get behind Carl!" Dave shouted. "You can't fight them without your armor!"

Poffo reluctantly did as Dave said, standing behind Carl to keep safe.

Of the four warriors on Dave's side, P1Go was putting up the best fight. The silver pig woman robot was swinging her sword so fast that it was a blur, blocking the blows from the piglin's axes, then slashing away at them until they went *POOF*. Her fighting style reminded Dave a lot of Robo-Steve's, and he felt a sharp pang in his chest when he remembered that his old friend was gone. He shook the thought of Robo-Steve from his head, remembering that he needed to concentrate and continue to fight on. It took all of Dave's concentration to block the axe blows, so he needed his wits about him.

Out of the corner of his eye, Dave could see the other four warriors fighting off the piglin brutes that were attacking from the other end of the hallway. Alex and Spidroth were swinging their swords at the piglin brutes, fighting them off as best they could. Dave was surprised to see that even Alex and Spidroth weren't able to take the piglin brutes down easily. Normally, the two women could cut down enemies as if they were nothing, but the brutes were fierce warriors.

Porkins and Saggo were behind Alex and Spidroth and had built themselves small towers, two blocks high. They stood on the towers, shooting arrows down at the brutes: Porkins from his bow and Saggo from her crossbow.

Dave turned back to focus on his own battle. A piglin brute swung its axe down at him, and Dave raised his diamond sword to meet the blow. Once he'd blocked the attack, Dave quickly swung his diamond sword back, then stabbed it forward at the brute's chest. The brute staggered backward, flashing red, then swung his axe at Dave once more. Dave ducked down, so the brute just swung at the air, then slashed his sword at the brute once more. When the blow connected this time, the brute exploded in a puff of smoke — *POOF*.

Some of the brutes had climbed up onto Carl's golem suit and were hacking away at it with their golden axes. Carl was doing his best to shake them off, but he'd had to duck down into the suit to protect his head, and he'd shoved Boggo into the suit as well, to protect the piglin. Dave was going to go over and help Carl, but before he could, Poffo ran forward, hitting the piglin brutes with his sword to get them off Carl. P1Go ran over as well, grabbing the brutes by the shoulders and yanking them off of Carl. Once all the brutes were off his golem suit, Carl reached into their head hole and pulled Boggo out, putting him back under his arm, then his little creeper head popped out. Carl charged forward towards the brutes once more, swinging his right arm and sending them flying.

Finally, almost all of the piglin brutes had been slain. The few that remained ran off, snorting angrily.

"You are traitors to Empress," one of the brutes said angrily. "When she returns, you be in big trouble!"

"Empress not coming back," said Saggo angrily. "Empress gone forever."

The brutes grunted, then disappeared back down the hallways. When they were gone, Dave and the others were alone once more.

"Come on," said Dave. "Let's get out of this castle before more of them turn up."

CHAPTER EIGHT

The Island

They wandered through the confusing maze of ruined black hallways until finally they found the exit. They walked out of the bastion remnant and found themselves in a biome full of red netherrack hills and lava. It looked just like the old Nether before it had changed. In the distance, Dave could see huge white ghasts floating in the sky and herds of red striders walking through the lava.

"A nether wastes biome," said P1G0.

"Back in my day, all the Nether was like this," said Porkins sadly.

P1G0 looked at him strangely.

"The Nether hasn't been like that for over a million years," said the robot. "Surely you can't be the old?"

"It's complicated," said Carl. "It involves a lot of weird time stuff."

"Wait," said P1G0, looking at Porkins, "you're a pigman, aren't you, sir? Just like Empress Chops?"

"That's enough talking," said Dave. "We need to get moving."

Dave knew that the subject of the old Nether and the Empress was a sensitive one for Porkins. He didn't want P1G0 to upset his friend by talking about the past.

"So how much further?" Spidroth asked as they walked along.

"Not long," said P1Go. "We should be at the laboratory in a couple of hours."

After they were a safe distance from the bastion remnant, they all sat down to have lunch. Or it might have been dinner or breakfast; Dave wasn't quite sure. As always, Carl ate baked potatoes, but instead of his usual two, he only ate one.

"Don't tell me you're finally running out of potatoes?" Dave asked him.

"I don't want to talk about it," said Carl grumpily.

Alex came over with some paper, and she and Carl started chatting, whispering to each other and drawing pictures.

"Are those fools still working on that comic?" Spidroth asked disapprovingly.

"It looks like it," said Dave. "Hey Carl," he shouted, "how's the comic going?"

"We're working on the chapter where Carl went down to the Phantom Realm to save you and Spidroth," said Alex.

"Er, I think you've got it the wrong way round," said Dave.

"I'm the main character in the book," said Carl. "We have to change some of the events to make sure I'm always the hero. It's just common sense."

"Ooo, and in our version of the story, Robo-Steve comes back from the Phantom Realm with you," said Alex. "I know it didn't happen in real life, but we're going to honor his memory by having him come back in the comic. Although when he comes back, he's going to get a cool new body."

"I was thinking jet black with red eyes," said Carl. "And his catchphrase is: 'I came back from the dead, and now you're going to get hit in the head.'"

"He says that to bad guys before he hits them in the head," Alex explained.

"That sounds nice," Dave smiled. "Not the hitting in the head part, but the Robo-Steve part."

"What is comic book?" asked Poffo, picking up one of Carl and Alex's pages.

"It's like a normal book, but it tells a story with pictures instead of words," said Alex. "Well, there are some words, but less than in a normal book. I don't really know how to explain it."

"Comic book look fun," said Poffo, studying the page. "Who is green worm in picture?"

"That's Carl," said Alex.

Poffo looked at the picture, then at Carl, and at the picture again, then at Carl again.

"Picture not good," said Poffo. "Does artist have small brain?"

"Give me that," said Carl, angrily grabbing the page off Poffo. "Some people just don't appreciate art."

Dave was having fun watching the others bicker, but he knew that they ought to get moving. Carl had climbed out of his golem suit, but Boggo was still underneath the golem's arm, squirming and *BURR*ing. Saggo was looking sadly at her husband-to-be. She looked like she wanted to cry.

"Come on, everyone," said Dave, standing up. "Let's go and save Boggo."

He put a hand on Saggo's shoulder. She looked up and smiled at him.

They resumed their journey, walking across the netherrack hills and making sure to keep well away from any ghasts. P1G0 said that zombified piglins often roamed the nether wastes biomes, but thankfully they didn't seem to be any nearby.

Dave found himself walking next to Saggo. She still looked sad, but there was a look of determination on her face as well.

"How are you doing, Saggo?" Dave asked her.

"Saggo okay," said Saggo. "Saggo just hope we can save Boggo. Saggo miss him."

"So, have you two been in love long?" Dave asked, trying to make conversation.

"Not long," said Saggo. "Saggo and Boggo got talking after you help us defeat Empress. Boggo very clever and very handsome, so Saggo fall in love."

"Er, how lovely," said Dave. 'Clever' and 'handsome' weren't words he would have used to describe Boggo, but maybe it was true by piglin standards.

"Saggo was sad after Saggo's brother died," said Saggo, "but meeting Boggo made Saggo happy again."

"Oh, I'm sorry to hear about your brother," said Dave.

"Conko was good piglin," said Saggo. "Empress forced him to be in army, then he went on mission and never came back. Saggo was very sad."

Dave knew that the Empress had been Porkins's friend once, but the more he heard about her, the more horrible a person she seemed. It seemed she'd shown no respect for the lives of the piglins at all, using them as her slaves and her soldiers without caring if they lived or died.

They came over a hill, and Dave saw a huge lava lake at the bottom of a valley, with an island in the middle. The island was covered in blue-green mushrooms and vegetation — another warped forest biome. In the middle of the forest was a tower made from gold, rising high above the mushrooms.

"That tower is the laboratory," said P1Go. "That's where the cure will be."

"Island should be safe," said Poffo confidently. "Warped forest biome is safe normally. Only bad guys are endermen, and those are safe if you don't look at them."

"I'm not so sure about that," said Carl, squinting. "I can see some things between the mushrooms that don't look like endermen. They look more like zombified piglins."

"But zombified piglins no live in warped forest!" said Poffo.

"Let's just all be careful," said Dave. "If the Empress had a laboratory here, there's no telling what weird things we might come across. We'll try and sneak through the forest to the laboratory without attracting any attention, but we may need to fight if we get spotted. Have your weapons ready at all times."

They made their way down the netherrack slope towards the lake. There was an old ruined bridge made from blackstone bricks that went from the shore to the island. Dave and the others crossed the bridge, keeping their eyes peeled in case they were attacked. Once they reached the forest, there was a cyan haze in the air, and blue-green vegetation in every direction: huge mushrooms the size of trees with cyan caps and purple stems with blue veins running through them, blue-green vines that twisted in spirals down from the mushroom heads, stringy roots growing up from the ground, and instead of grass the ground was covered in a squishy blue-green material.

Dave led the way as they all walked through the crimson forest, taking care to be as quiet as possible.

"Have you seen any more zombified piglins?" Dave whispered to Carl.

"Yeah, I can see a few in the distance, hidden by the vegetation," Carl whispered back. "Thankfully, it doesn't look as if they've spotted us yet."

The only positive about there being zombified piglins in the forest seemed to be that they had scared off all the endermen – or, at least, Dave never saw any endermen. As they got nearer to the center of the island, even Dave, whose eyes were nowhere near as sharp as Carl's, spotted some zombified piglins through the overgrowth. The nearer they got to the laboratory, the more zombified piglins there seem to be.

Finally, they could see the golden tower up ahead of them, through the vines and mushrooms. At the foot of the gold tower was an iron door with a button next to it. Unfortunately, there were also lots of zombified piglins wandering aimlessly about around the tower.

"We can take those zombies on," said Alex. "There's only about fifteen of them."

"The trouble is, once those ones see us and start snorting, all the other zombified piglins in the forest will know we're here too," said Dave.

"Good point," said Alex sadly.

"We need a distraction," said Spidroth. "Carl, you need to distract the zombified piglins."

"Er, what?" said Carl.

"In your golem suit, you're the fastest out of all of us," explained Spidroth. "You can easily outrun those zombies, and you can lead them away from the bottom of the tower. Then the rest of us will be able to enter without getting spotted."

"So, you want to sacrifice me to the zombies, do you?" said Carl. "That's just great."

"Don't be such a fool," snapped Spidroth. "Once you have escaped from the zombified piglins, you can run back around and join us at the tower. With the speed your suit can go, it should be easy. Or, if you'd prefer, I can put the golem suit on instead and show you how it's done."

"Okay, okay, I'll do it," said Carl, rolling his eyes. "But if it all goes wrong and I get killed, I'll be waiting in the Phantom Realm to beat you up."

"Fool," snapped Spidroth.

"All right, calm down, you two," said Dave. "That does seem like a good idea. You sure you're all right doing that, Carl?"

"Yeah, I guess so," said Carl, "but someone is going to have to carry Boggo."

"My strength is superior to the average organic being," said P1Go. "I can carry him if you like, sir."

Carl took Boggo from under his arm and handed him to the robot. She held him in her arms like a big ugly baby.

"*ROOK,*" said Boggo.

"*ROOK* to you too," said Carl. "Right, wish me luck. And if I die, I want you all to know that you're big idiots."

"Thanks, Carl," said Alex cheerily.

Carl rolled his eyes, then began walking towards the golden tower. Dave and the others watched from behind some giant mushrooms as the creeper walked up to the tower in his golem suit.

"Hey, zombie idiots!" Carl shouted, waving his arms to get the zombified piglins' attention. "Delicious creeper here, all ready to be eaten. Come and get it!"

Immediately, all the zombified piglins in the area began rushing towards Carl. Carl legged it back into the warped forest, running off in a different direction from where Dave and the others were hiding. As he ran, more and more zombified piglins began to chase him until a whole horde of them were behind him.

I hope he doesn't trip up, Dave thought to himself, as Carl and the zombified piglins all disappeared into the forest, hidden by the vegetation.

"Right, come on, this is our chance," said Dave. "The tower is unguarded, so let's go in and get that cure for Boggo."

"*BURR,*" said Boggo.

CHAPTER NINE

The Laboratory

They ran up to the golden tower. Dave pressed his hand on the button, and the iron door swung open. They all ran inside, and the door slammed shut behind them.

The floors, walls and ceiling of the laboratory were all made from gold blocks. There were some shroomlight blocks in the ceiling to light up the room. Around the edges of the room were crafting blocks that Dave was familiar with, such as crafting tables, furnaces and anvils, but there were also lots of strange computers and devices that he didn't recognize. He supposed they must all be things that the Empress had built. There were two stairways as well, one leading up and the other leading down. Since they were on the ground floor, Dave supposed that the tower must have a basement as well, or maybe several floors of basements.

Suddenly, the door swung open, and Carl squeezed through the doorway into the room. The door slammed shut behind him.

"I've lost the zombies," said Carl. "We should be safe. Probably."

"I hope you did it properly," said Spidroth, giving Carl a suspicious look. "If you messed up and led them back here..."

"I'm sure Carl did do it properly," said Dave, quickly saying something

50

before Carl and Spidroth started arguing again. "Now, P1G0, where can we find this cure?"

The robot went over to one of the computer terminals and placed her robotic hand into a hole. Suddenly her eyes went from pink to green and began flickering. After a few seconds, her eyes turned back to normal, and she pulled her hand out of the hole.

"What was all that about?" Carl asked.

"I was interfacing with the local computer," said P1G0. "It seems that the cure is on the bottom floor of the tower — floor minus five."

"Minus five?!" said Carl. "Are you telling me there are five floors below us?"

"yes, I am," said P1G0.

Dave didn't like the idea of going deep underground in this tower, but it seemed like they had no choice.

They made their way down the stairs. The stairway was lit by shroomlights embedded into the walls. They passed another floor of the laboratory, which was set out in a very similar way to the one above, but there were huge bones scattered about the floor — rib cages that were far too big to be any creature that Dave had ever seen. He had seen fossils like this before, though, scattered across the Nether.

They went down another floor, then another, then passed a floor where the lights had broken so they couldn't see anything, then finally they reached the bottom floor. The shroomlights on this floor were flickering, giving the laboratory a creepy quality. Dave had a shock when he saw what he thought were bits of bodies on some tables, but on closer inspection, they turned out to be bits of robots. The robots looked just like P1G0 — silver pigmen.

"This place is giving me the creeps," said Carl, picking up a severed robot head and looking at it.

Suddenly a green image flickered into life in the middle of the room. Dave had seen an image like this before — it was a hologram. The hologram appeared to be of an elderly pig woman. She looked ancient and was using a walking stick.

"Chops," said Porkins sadly, looking at the hologram.

"I have been trapped in the Nether now for sixty-five years," said the hologram. "Despite my best efforts, I am unable to return to the Overworld. It seems that the Nether is still fast-forwarding, and until it slows down, travel to the Overworld will be impossible. I've tried building portals across the Nether to see if the fast-forwarding is only limited to some areas, but it seems that all of the Nether is in the same situation. I have no choice but to wait and build up my army. I have devised a computer system that allows anyone on the planet to be tracked, so as soon as the Nether stops fast-forwarding, I will be able to track down that traitor Porkins and the others who may be a threat to my plans. Once they are dealt with, my invasion of the Overworld will begin. Villagers and illagers alike will regret the way they treated the pigmen."

The image flickered and then disappeared.

"It's some kind of hologram diary," said Spidroth.

"Poor Chops," said Porkins. "She was so consumed by hatred. I can't believe she fell so far."

The hologram flickered into life again, but this time the elderly pig woman was sitting in a chair. Judging by her wrinkled face, she was much older than before, and bits of her body had been replaced by robotic parts. Her legs were both robot legs, and one of her arms was completely robotic too. The arm that wasn't robotic was withered and rested weakly on her lap.

"I have now been trapped in this forsaken place for one hundred and ten years," the hologram of the pig woman said bitterly. "I have had to use technology to prolong my life, but each year my body gets weaker. My empire

52

is getting stronger though, and I now have fortresses all across the Nether. I will wait as long as it takes for the Nether to stop fast-forwarding, and when it does, I will have my vengeance!"

"She waited all that time to have her revenge, and then she messed it up," said Carl. "What a loser."

"Be quiet, Carl!" Porkins snapped. Dave was surprised — the pigman never normally got angry about anything.

The hologram flickered again, and this time the elderly pig woman was replaced by the version of the Empress that Dave had seen before — a grey floating skull surrounded by white blaze rods.

"It has been over half a million years now," the Empress hissed. "Without these hologram diaries, I believe I would have gone insane by now. I have no one to talk to. The piglins are all fools, and my robots are all sycophants who just do whatever I say. I feel my mind slipping, but I must keep going. I have tried everything to keep my body and my mind alive, and this form seems to be the best one so far. Blazes were developed by the Old People, who had far superior technology to our own. By combining my body with the blazes, I should no longer age. I miss having arms and legs, but I have my robots and my piglins to do things for me. It has been so long, but my mind is still focused on my revenge. When the time comes, I will have my vengeance. All the pain I've gone through will be nothing compared to what I do to the Overworld. Nothing!"

The hologram flickered off once more. They waited to see if it would turn on again, but it seemed to have finished.

"That was when she'd been in the Nether for half a million years," said Spidroth. "So it was another half a million years before we met her again. She must have been so lonely."

Dave was surprised to see Spidroth feeling such sympathy for someone

else, but then he remembered that she had been in a similar situation —
trapped in the void beneath the bedrock for countless years.

"Okay, this is all getting very gloomy," said Carl. "Where is the cure for
Boggo?"

"Here," said P1Go. The silver pigman robot was standing next to a chest
with a bottle of bubbling purple potion in her hand. "A couple of drops of this
should turn Boggo back to normal."

"Then what we waiting for?" said Saggo, running over. P1Go had left
Boggo on the ground, sitting up against the wall. He was staring around
blankly, making the occasional snorting sound.

Saggo took the bottle from P1Go, then knelt down next to Boggo. He
looked at her with blank eyes.

"Burr?" he said, sounding confused.

"Poffo, please hold Boggo's mouth open," said Saggo.

Poffo came over, knelt down next to Boggo, and used his trotters to hold
Boggo's mouth open. Then Saggo tilted the bottle, letting a few drops of
purple liquid fall into Boggo's mouth.

The change was almost immediate. Boggo started vibrating, and the
green mold on his flesh began to disappear. Then pink flesh began to grow
back over his exposed bits of bone until finally, he was back to normal again.

"Boggo had strange dream," said the piglin, rubbing his head.

"Oh, Boggo!" said Saggo, giving him a big hug.

"Aw, isn't it romantic?" said Alex.

"I suppose so," said Carl. "If you like that sort of thing."

Dave met Spidroth's gaze, but then the two of them quickly looked away
from each other. Dave could feel his cheeks burning.

"Carl!" said Boggo, noticing the creeper for the first time. "Have you
written best man speech for Boggo's wedding yet?"

"Written the speech?" said Carl incredulously. "No, I haven't; I've been too busy saving your life!"

"Thank you for saving Boggo's life, but don't forget to write speech," said Boggo. "Best man speech should be highlight of wedding, with good jokes and lots of emotion. But make sure it's not better than Boggo's speech. This is Boggo's wedding, so Boggo needs to be star."

Dave had a horrible vision of having to sit through hours and hours of piglins giving speeches. It was not a happy thought.

"Come on, it's time we were going," said Spidroth.

"Yes, we must get back in time for wedding," said Saggo.

"What time is the wedding?" Alex asked. "How do you tell time the Nether, anyway?"

"Piglins not very good at telling time," said Poffo. "That's why piglins always late for things."

"Yes," said Saggo. "Wedding should actually have been three days ago, but Boggo kept changing his mind about his suit."

"Boggo couldn't figure out whether he looked better in black or navy," said Boggo.

"Do you mean we've been rushing around this whole time, and the wedding was delayed anyway?" asked Carl. He rolled his eyes.

They made their way back up the stairs until they reached the ground floor again.

"Someone should check to see if there are any zombified piglins out there," said Carl.

"I'll do it," said Spidroth, walking up to the iron door. She pressed the button next to it, and the door swung open. She looked around the door, then pulled her head back. The door slammed shut.

"Well?" asked Carl. "Are there any there?"

"Yes," said Spidroth, her cheeks going pale. "By my estimate, at least three hundred, maybe more. The tower is completely surrounded."

CHAPTER TEN

The Staircase

They made their way up the staircases to the top of the golden tower. When they got there, they climbed out of a trapdoor onto the roof and looked out across the island. There were hundreds of zombified piglins surrounding them in every direction, all of them standing perfectly still.

"Is it just me, or do the zombified piglins look a lot more organized than they were before?" Carl asked.

"I hate to say it, but you're right," said Spidroth. "Before, they were just a mindless horde, attacking anything they saw. But now it seems like they're waiting for us."

Looking down at the zombified piglins, Dave noticed something strange. One of them didn't look right — standing a few rows back from the golden tower was a normal piglin. He seemed to be holding something, but Dave couldn't make out what it was.

"Carl, look at that piglin down there," said Dave, pointing. "Is that a normal piglin rather than a zombie? And what is it holding?"

Carl squinted. Then his eyes went wide with surprise.

"Yep, it's a normal piglin all right," he said, "and he's holding a staff. A golden staff with an emerald on the top."

Dave's mouth dropped open in shock.

"You mean..."

"Yeah," said Carl, "it looks just like the one that Herobrine gave to Trotter. The one he used to control the zombie pigmen."

"But that staff was destroyed," said Porkins. "Didn't it go in the lava and explode?"

"It did," said Dave, "but what was to stop Herobrine building another one?"

"Fascinating," said P1Go. "If someone has been controlling zombified piglins with magic, that would explain why they've been acting so strangely lately."

"This is very confusing," said Boggo, scratching his head with a trotter. "Boggo's brain hurt."

Suddenly the normal piglin looked up, spotting them.

"Oh no," said Alex, "I think we been seen."

"Well, at least we're safe here," said Dave.

The normal piglin slammed the golden staff on the ground, and the emerald began to glow green. Suddenly the zombified piglins all began to move, getting on each other's shoulders and forming some kind of structure.

"They're building stairs!" said Alex.

Dave realized she was right: zombified piglins had arranged themselves into a staircase, getting higher and higher every second. Finally, the staircase was finished, and the top of it reached the roof of the golden tower. The normal piglin began walking up the staircase towards them.

"Anyone got some TNT?" asked Carl. "Let's blow this weird staircase to bits and that piglin with the staff too."

"No, wait!" said Saggo, looking over the top of the tower. "Don't hurt that piglin!"

"Why not?" Carl asked.

"Because it's my brother!" shouted Saggo. "It's Conko!"

CHAPTER ELEVEN

The Leader

The normal piglin reached the top of the staircase. He was wearing netherite armor, apart from his helmet was missing, and his eyes were glowing green.

"Conko!" shouted Saggo. She ran forward towards her brother, but he aimed the golden staff at her and sent her flying backward with a flash of green energy. She landed in Boggo's arms.

"Why Conko hurt sister?" Boggo asked angrily.

Conko smirked. He ignored the piglins and instead turned to Dave.

"Hello, Dave," said Conko, in a very un-piglin-like voice.

Dave's blood went cold; he'd heard that voice before: it was a voice he hoped he'd never have to hear again.

"Herobrine!" he gasped.

Spidroth drew her red sword. "I don't know how you've returned, father," she snarled at Conko, "but I will strike you down right now!"

"Relax, daughter," grinned Conko. "I'm not really Herobrine. Well, I am sort of. I'm a *shade*."

"I don't want to sound stupid, but what's a shade?" Carl asked.

"He is a copy of Herobrine," said Spidroth angrily. "Or at least a copy of Herobrine's personality. Back when his empire stretched across the world,

Herobrine used to put his mind into other beings, so he could rule from afar. The beings were an exact copy of Herobrine's personality at that exact moment. He couldn't manipulate them from afar or see what was happening to them, but because they had his personality, he knew that they would do things the way he wanted."

"So Herobrine made a copy of his personality and put it in the brain of this poor piglin?" asked Alex.

"Correct," Conko grinned. "This fool of a piglin was part of the army that the Empress sent to capture me. I slew his comrades and then took the information I needed from him. I was going to slay him as well, but then I saw a better use for him. I gave him this staff and told him to start gathering together all the zombie pigmen in the Nether. Then, if I ever needed them, I would have an army ready and waiting for me."

"Those chaps aren't zombie pigmen," said Porkins angrily, aiming his bow at Conko. "They're zombified piglins."

"Well, whatever you want to call them, they're my army," said Conko, shrugging.

"Not anymore," growled Spidroth, "I'm going to cut you down!"

She dashed forward, lifting her red sword, ready to strike it down on Conko.

"No!" Saggo shrieked.

Spidroth stopped just in time, her blade just above Conko's forehead. She looked like she wanted to strike Conko down more than anything, and it was taking all her own willpower to stop her.

"You've become soft, daughter," Conko said, smiling mockingly at Spidroth. "The old you would have struck me down no matter whose body I was wearing."

"Listen, you Herobrine copy or whatever you are," said Carl, "the real

Herobrine is gone. He's trapped in a dead dimension with no way out, so there's no point in you gathering a big army for him. He's not coming back."

"You lie," said Conko. His smile disappeared for the first time, replaced by a scowl.

"It's the truth, father," said Spidroth. "You have been banished from this universe for good. You are the only remnant of Herobrine that is left — a cheap copy in a weak body."

"Is that so?" Conko growled. "If that is true, then I will launch a new empire with this body. This piglin may be weak, but I can enhance him with magic and make him strong."

"Get out of Saggo's brother's body," Saggo sobbed. "Get out, you big meanie!"

"This has been fun, but I will leave you now," said Conko. "I spotted you all earlier in the blue forest, so I waited until you got inside the golden tower and then ordered my soldiers to surround it. In this body, I may be too weak to defeat you all, but there are over a thousand of these disgusting zombie creatures on this island. They will wait here as long as it takes. Either you will starve inside that tower, or you'll try to escape, and they will slay you. And don't even think about digging underground, as this island's surface is only two blocks thick. Below that is lava. You're trapped, I'm afraid. Of course, I could order my soldiers to let you leave, but only on one condition."

"And what condition is that?" Dave asked.

"You tell me how to find end portals," said Conko.

Dave laughed.

"What's so funny about that?" growled Conko.

"Oh, it's just that I told the real Herobrine that already," said Dave. "Well, I didn't tell him exactly, but he sucked the information from my brain. If he knew that information, how come you don't know?"

"It's because this shade only has Herobrine's memories from the point that it was created," said Spidroth.

Conko looked angry.

"If the real me got the information about how to reach the End, how is the universe still here?"

He seemed to be talking more to himself than anyone else.

"Maybe the egg didn't do what it was supposed to," Conko muttered. He looked almost afraid. "But if that's true, this has all been for nothing!"

Conko looked up at them with madness in his eyes.

"You," he scowled, looking at Dave. "You wretched villager! Ever since I heard your name, my life has been one problem after another. But it all ends now!"

Conko pulled out a netherite sword and dashed forward towards Dave. Dave was so shocked that he didn't even have time to pull out his own sword. Conko swung his blade through the air, aiming at Dave's chest.

POW!

Carl stepped forward and punched Conko, sending the piglin tumbling down the zombified piglin staircase.

"Conko!" Saggo yelled, running down the staircase after her brother. Boggo and Poffo ran down after her.

"Does anyone else think that staircase doesn't look very safe?" said Carl.

"Come on," said Dave, running down the staircase after the piglins. It was a very weird experience, running down a staircase made from creatures that were still alive — if you could call zombified piglins *alive* — and every time Dave stepped on one of the zombified piglin stairs, they looked at him and made *BURR* noises.

At the bottom of the stairs, Conko was lying on the ground with Saggo kneeling next to him. He looked dazed, and the golden staff had fallen onto the ground. All the zombified piglins were standing around, perfectly still as if awaiting orders. Dave picked up the golden staff.

"Get away, all of you," he said, pointing the staff at the zombified piglins. The emerald on the top glowed green, and then all the zombies began walking away. The zombies that made up the staircase began dismantling the structure as well, climbing off of each other's shoulders. Carl, Spidroth, Alex, Porkins and P1Go reach the bottom of the staircase just in time before the structure collapsed and all the zombified piglins began walking off back into the forest.

"How are you, brother?" Saggo asked Conko. "Please be okay."

Dave noticed that Conko's eyes were no longer glowing green.

"The shade has left him," said Spidroth. "His fall must have knocked the copy of Herobrine's mind from his brain."

"So, is it gone for good?" Dave asked, looking around them as if expecting to see a ghostly image of Herobrine somewhere.

"Yes," said Spidroth. Herobrine's shades cannot move from body to body — once they are removed from a vessel, or the vessel they are in is destroyed, they disappear as well."

Dave was glad to hear that. The last thing they needed was a copy of Herobrine taking over someone else's mind.

"Saggo?" said Conko, looking up at his sister. "Is that you? Conko had very strange dream."

"Oh, Conko!" said Saggo, reaching down and giving her brother a hug.

"Why Saggo wearing wedding dress?" asked Conko. "And who is stylish piglin in suit?"

"Conko, meet Boggo," said Saggo. "Boggo is going to be Saggo's husband. Wedding is today."

"Conko like weddings," said Conko happily. "Conko got cool dance moves, so Conko always get lots of kisses from girls."

Saggo and Boggo helped Conko to his feet. He was a bit unsteady at first, then he seemed to be okay.

Porkins pulled out a diamond shovel and quickly dug a hole two blocks deep into the ground. At the bottom of the hole was lava.

"What did you do that for, you weirdo?" Carl asked.

"To do this, dear boy," said Porkins, taking the golden staff off of Dave. He held the staff over the hole then dropped it. It landed in the lava, sunk down below the surface and then there was a *KRAKOOM* as it exploded, spraying bits of lava from the hole. Thankfully no one got hit by the spray.

As they walked back through the warped forest island, Dave noticed some zombified piglins roaming about. They were no longer running around like vicious beasts or standing rigidly to attention; instead, they were roaming about aimlessly.

"It seems like the zombified piglins are back to normal now," said P1Go.

"That's a relief," said Alex.

"It will certainly make getting back a lot easier," agreed Dave. "I think I'm just going to build a bed and lie down when we get back to the wedding. I'm exhausted."

"Dave no lie down," said Saggo angrily, bashing Dave on the head with a trotter. "At Saggo's wedding everyone has to dance!"

"Okay, okay," said Dave, rubbing his head. "But I warn you, I'm not a good dancer."

"Poffo show Dave some moves," said Poffo proudly. "Poffo will help Dave get all the ladies, just like Poffo."

"Er, thanks, Poffo," said Dave. "That sounds great."

"Oh, does it?" said Spidroth, raising an eyebrow at him.

"Er, I didn't mean like that," said Dave, feeling his cheeks glowing red. "I just meant it would be good to learn some dance moves."

"Hmmph," said Spidroth, walking on ahead of him.

"I don't think she's going to agree to marry you any time soon after that," Carl whispered to Dave, putting a hand on his shoulder.

"Carl!" said Dave, shoving the creeper's hand away.

"Are you all right, Dave?" Carl asked with a grin. "Your cheeks have gone very red."

CHAPTER TWELVE

The Wedding

The journey back was a lot easier, now that they no longer had to worry about vicious hordes of zombified piglins. They took a long way around to avoid going through the bastion remnant again and managed to avoid passing through the basalt dealta biome as well. All those detours meant the journey took a lot longer, but at least it was safe. The only trouble they had was from a few ghasts, but Dave and his friends managed to take them down easily with their bows.

When they finally made it back to the warped forest where the wedding was taking place, everyone had gone apart from an elderly piglin with a grey beard who was asleep on one of the chairs.

Saggo shook the elderly piglin awake.

"Grandpa, where is everyone?" Saggo asked him.

"Hello, Saggo," said the piglin, "everyone got bored waiting, so went home. They thought wedding was canceled."

"Poffo, tell everyone wedding is not canceled," Saggo said. "Tell them wedding is happening now."

Poffo nodded, then ran off. Before long, there were piglins everywhere, all chatting and taking their seats on the two aisles of chairs that had been set out. Dave and his friends took a seat near the back.

"Have you written your best man's speech yet, Carl?" Alex asked.

"Of course I haven't," said Carl. "When have I had time to write that stupid speech with all the adventuring we've been doing?"

"Don't worry," said Alex, handing Carl a piece of paper. "I've written one for you. It's packed full of fantastic jokes and heartfelt comments about Boggo and Saggo."

"Er, thanks, Alex," said Carl. He was about to read the piece of paper, but then a hush fell over the congregation as a piglin in purple robes stepped onto the stage at the front. Boggo was standing at the front too, Dave saw, wearing his wedding suit and top hat.

Music began to play from somewhere, and Dave noticed a piglin standing next to a jukebox by the side of the stage. The music playing didn't seem very appropriate for a wedding – it was good music, though, with a nice beat.

"Pigstep is cool tune," one of the piglins near Dave whispered to their neighbor as they bobbed their heads in time to the music.

Suddenly everyone turned their heads. Dave turned and saw Saggo walking down the aisle in her wedding dress, which had been given a good clean after their adventures in the Nether. P1Go had linked arms with her and was leading her down the aisle.

"Saggo look so beautiful," a piglin near Dave muttered.

"Boggo is lucky piglin," said another.

"Are you crying, Alex?" Carl whispered.

"It's just so romantic," said Alex, using the sleeve of her black ninja outfit to wipe away her tears.

"Pah," said Spidroth.

"Don't pretend you wouldn't like to get married too," Carl teased. "And we all know who you'd like to get married to!"

Spidroth slapped Carl on the side of the head.

"Ow," the little creeper said. "What was that for?"

Saggo reached the front and walked onto the stage, standing opposite Boggo. Boggo reached forward, taking her trotter's in his own.

"Piglin brothers and sisters, we gathered here today for wedding of Boggo and Saggo," said the piglin in purple robes. "Boggo, do you take Saggo to be wife?"

"Boggo do," said Boggo.

"And Saggo, do you take Boggo to be husband?"

"Saggo do," said Saggo.

"Then, by power invested in Zordo, Zordo now pronounce you piglin and wife."

A great cheer went up, all the piglins clapping and shouting happily. Despite himself, Dave found himself caught up in the moment, and even he was clapping and cheering along with the rest of them. Even Spidroth had a slight smile on her face, Dave was pleased to see. She looked almost emotional.

Next came the meal. Everyone sat down around tables, and piglin waiters served the food. There were several courses, although the only ingredients in every dish were pork chops and mushrooms. Dave supposed that there wasn't much variety of food in the Nether compared to the Overworld. Across the table, he saw Carl take a sneaky bite of one of the potatoes he had in his golem suit.

After the meal, it was time for speeches. Saggo's father gave a lovely speech about how happy he was that his daughter was now married and that his son Conko had returned, then it was time for Boggo to give a speech. He stood up, and the guests all fell silent.

"Boggo thank you all for coming today," said Boggo. "This special day for

Boggo, as Boggo get to marry his soulmate Saggo. When Boggo first meet Saggo, Boggo think she very pretty piglin, but then Boggo get to know her and realize she is also funny and kind and good friend to Boggo. Then Boggo fall in love."

"Are you all right, Alex?" Porkins whispered.

"I always cry at weddings," said Alex, dabbing her eyes and blowing her nose on her sleeve.

Dave saw Spidroth rolling her eyes at Alex.

"Boggo would also like to thank friends from Overworld," Boggo continued. "Carl and his friends were a big help to piglins, helping us defeat Empress, and now we free." He raised his cup. "To Carl and friends!"

All the other piglins turned towards Dave and his friends, raising their own cups.

"To Carl and friends!" they all repeated.

"And now Boggo's speech is finished," said Boggo. "Boggo would like to invite Boggo's best man and best friend to do speech now. Everyone clap for Carl!"

Everyone clapped. Carl pushed back his chair and stood up in his golem suit. He looked uncharacteristically nervous. He picked up the piece of paper that Alex had given him and began to read.

"Er, having a good marriage is a lot like being a good ninja," Carl read. He gave Alex a furious look, but she just grinned back at him and gave him a thumbs up. Carl took a deep breath and then continued to read. "It takes discipline, patience and sometimes enemies will throw shurikens at your head."

The piglins all gave him confused looks. Carl scrunched up Alex's speech and threw it on the floor.

"Right," said Carl, "I don't know much about marriage. In creeper culture, there is no marriage. My mother was a creeper queen with over one hundred thousand children, so I never really knew her. In fact, all my relationships were a bit strange growing up, as everyone I knew eventually blew themselves up. But then I met my friends Dave and Porkins, and later some other friends too. They gave me the family I never had before and showed me what a good family could be like. From what I've seen of Boggo and Saggo, I think they're going to be a good family as well. Saggo risked her life to save Boggo, and if that's not true love, I don't know what is. And Boggo may be an idiot, and he may have destroyed my awesome diamond golem armor, but he's a nice guy, and I know he'll treat Saggo well. Anyway, that's enough rambling on from me. Everyone raise your cups — to Boggo and Saggo!"

"Boggo and Saggo!" everyone repeated.

Carl quickly sat down, and everyone resumed talking.

"Great speech, Carl," said Dave, putting a hand on his friend's shoulder.

"You didn't do any jokes, Carl," said Alex, looking disappointed. "I had loads of good jokes written in my speech. There was one about how piglins look a lot like pigs. It was pretty funny."

"Er, I'm sure it was," said Carl.

Boggo walked over and gave Carl a hug.

"Thank you, best friend Carl!" said Boggo happily. "That speech very great! Although needed more jokes. Best man speech supposed to be funny."

"I tried to tell him," shrugged Alex.

Next, it was time for the dancing. The piglins cleared away the tables, then they put a music disc on the jukebox, and all began to dance. The dancing was jolly and upbeat, with piglins linking arms and swinging each other round and round. Alex and Porkins enthusiastically joined in the dancing, and after some persuading, Dave got up and joined as well. Carl and

Spidroth both refused to get involved.

"I have a reputation as a cool dude to maintain," Carl explained to Dave. "Cool dudes don't dance; they just stand at the side of the dancefloor and look cool. Everyone knows that."

"Dancing is for fools," said Spidroth.

Dave had never been much of a dancer, but before long, he found himself having lots of fun, dancing with partner after partner. He danced with more piglins than he could count, including Saggo, Poffo, Boggo and even P1Go. The robot was a surprisingly good dancer.

"I am programmed to be able to pick up any skill through observation," the robot told Dave. "After watching a couple of dances, my systems updated, and I became an expert."

Dave also danced with Porkins a couple of times and Alex. Alex was so full of life when she danced that it made Dave laugh. She swung him around so fast that he got dizzy and almost fell over.

"Isn't dancing fun?" Alex asked happily.

"Yeah, it is," said Dave. He looked over and saw Spidroth and Carl, both of them standing stony-faced on the edge of the dancefloor.

I wish Spidroth would come over and dance, Dave thought to himself.

Alex was just spinning Dave around again when suddenly the music disc changed, and a slow song came on. All the piglins began to dance in a slow waltz, so Dave and Alex followed suit. Dave put his arm on Alex's back, and the two of them were looking right into each other's eyes. He'd never noticed before how green Alex's eyes were. They were as green as emeralds.

Even though he was facing away from her, Dave could suddenly feel Spidroth's eyes boring into his back.

"Er, I think that's enough dancing for me," said Dave quickly, letting go of Alex.

"Oh, okay," said Alex, sounding disappointed.

Dave quickly walked over and joined Spidroth and Carl.

"Having fun, were we?" Spidroth asked Dave.

"Er, yes, although I'm a bit exhausted from all the dancing now," Dave aid. "I think I'm just going to sit down for a while."

"You do whatever you want to do," said Spidroth.

Carl looked at Spidroth and Dave, but for once, he didn't say anything.)ave was very thankful for that.

Eventually, the piglins got tired and sat down around the tables, which ad been rebuilt on the edge of the dancefloor. Alex and Porkins, both xhausted and covered in sweat, came over and rejoined Dave, Spidroth and 'arl.

"That was terrific fun," said Porkins, sitting down. "I haven't had a jolly ;ood laugh like that in a long time!"

"I suppose we ought to be going," Dave said.

"I suppose so, old chap," said Porkins, sounding a bit disappointed.

They all went over to Boggo and Saggo, who were sitting together holding iands.

"We're all going to go now, back to the Overworld," said Carl. "Great vedding, you guys."

"Thank you, Carl," said Saggo. "But how come Carl wasn't dancing :arlier?"

"Unfortunately, I'm allergic to dancing," said Carl. "If I try to dance, I :ome out in a rash."

"Oh dear," said Saggo. "Poor Carl."

"Aren't you going to stay to see fireworks?" Boggo asked.

"I'm afraid not," said Dave. "We really must be getting back."

"Thanks for everything, Carl and Carl's friends," said Boggo. "You are all

73

good friends to the piglins."

"I'm sure we'll all meet again soon," said Dave.

After saying a few more goodbyes, to Poffo, P1G0 and some of the other piglins they knew, Dave and his friends all walked away from the wedding. In a grove in the middle of some tall cyan mushrooms, Dave built another portal and lit it.

"Well, that's another crazy adventure in the Nether done with," said Carl. "Let's hope we never have to come here ever again."

"Oh, don't be so miserable, Carl," said Alex. "I had a great time!"

"Have you forgotten how we were almost slain by magma cubes falling from the sky?" Carl asked.

"Well, I guess that bit wasn't so fun," said Alex. "But the dancing was great."

"Yes," said Spidroth, raising an eyebrow and giving Alex a suspicious stare. "You certainly looked like you were having fun, Alex."

"Er, let's all get out of here," said Dave.

He walked up to the purple rippling force field, then stepped through it back into the Overworld.

EPILOGUE

It was nighttime in Bedrock City. Torrents of rain splashed down on the ancient buildings, and the moon was covered by clouds.

Mad Mulligan sat at the top of an old tower, eating porkchops. The part of the tower he was in looked like it had housed a bell once, but the bell was long gone. There was a roof over his head and views in every direction. He knew from past experience that this tower was the best lookout point in the city: it sat at a cross junction and overlooked all the main roads.

Mulligan had a sudden vision; Dave and his friends had returned from the Nether and had resumed their journey once more. Mulligan didn't have a plan for what he would do once Dave reached Bedrock City. He knew that if he planned ahead, Dave would predict his actions with the Sight. No, he would have to come up with a plan on the spot and improvise. That would be the only way to defeat Dave.

I shouldn't have taught him how to use the Sight, Mulligan thought bitterly. He'd been too cocky and confident, and now he was paying the price. He'd lost all his rare magical trinkets and weapons when he'd fallen in the lava, so now all he had were his wits.

This will be my ultimate test, Mulligan thought to himself. *I'm gonna have to defeat a foe who has the same powers as me. It won't be easy.*

Still, Mulligan had never shied away from a challenge. He was confident that whatever happened when Dave reached Bedrock City, he would win out in the end. He would defeat the villager and his friends and then claim the ender dragon for his own. But for now, there was nothing to do but keep his strength up. He took another bite of his porkchop, and he waited...

To be continued...

Made in the USA
Monee, IL
06 April 2021